ZEN GARDENS

Kyoto's Nature Enclosed

MITSUMURA SUIKO SHOIN

CONTENTS (The Location of Gardens and Transportation Guide)

35	Entoku-in	Simo Kawaramachi Dori Yasaka Torii Mae Sagaru Higashiyama-ku	Take the ♯206 Municipal bus and get off at Higashiyama Yasui.
36	Kôdai-ji	Simo Kawaramachi Dori Yasaka Torii Mae Sagaru Higashiyama-ku	Take the ♯206 Municipal bus and get off at Higashiyama Yasui.
37. 38	Tenryû-ji	Saga Tenryû-ji Susukino Baba-cho 68, Ukyo-ku	Take the JR San'in Line and get off at Saga Station.
39. 40	Tôji-in	Tôji-in Kitamachi 63, Kita-ku	Take the ♯52 Municipal bus and get off at Tôji-in Higashi Machi.
41~43	Saihô-ji	Matsuo Kamigaya-cho 56, Nishikyo-ku	Take the ♯73 Kyoto bus and get off at Kokedera michi.
44	Jizô-in	Yamada Kitano-cho 23, Nishikyo-ku	Take the ♯73 Kyoto bus and get off at Kokedera Michi.
45	Shôden-ji	Nishigamo Chinju-an-cho 112, Kita-ku	Take the ♯9 Municipal bus and get off at Jinkô-in mae.
46	Konpuku-ji	Ichijô-jj Saigata-cho 20, Sakyo-ku	Take the ♯5 Municipal bus and get off at Ichijô-ji Sagarimatsu.
47	Shisen-dô	Ichijô-ji Monguchi-cho 27, Sakyo-ku	Take the ♯5 Municipal bus and get off at Ichijô-ji Sagarimatsu.

The above directions on transportation begin from Kyoto Station

ZEN GARDENS

First Edition Dec. 1990
Fifth Edition Oct. 1994
by Mitsumura Suiko Shoin Co., Ltd.
Shinsantora Bldg. 4F Omiya-dori Shijo-sagaru Shimogyo-ku,
Kyoto 600 Japan

Photographs : ©1990 Mizuno Katsuhiko
Text : ©1990 Tom Wright
Editor : Mitsumura Suiko Shoin Co., Ltd.

©1990 Kinzo Honda Printed in Japan

ISBN4-8381-0111-2

ZEN GARDENS

禅の庭

1．大徳寺方丈東庭
江戸時代　枯山水
二重刈込の生垣を背景に七五三の石
組を低く配している。直線様の構成
だが流動的な感覚で組まれている。

1. Daitoku-ji
Edo period ; *karesansui* (dry landscape garden)
In front of a higher fuller shrubbery is a lower well trimmed hedge delineating the eastern edge of the enclosure. Looking across a forest of moss from the *hojo* (abbot's quarters), the stonework is set in groupings of seven, five and three, felicitous numbers in Japanese mythology.

2. 大徳寺方丈南庭
江戸時代　枯山水
二つの砂盛を置いた白砂の中、苔に
囲まれた石は島を表す。唐門の左奥、
大刈込と豪壮な枯滝石組が有名。

2. Daitoku-ji
Edo period ; dry landscape garden
Amidst two mounds of white sand is a
rock surrounded by moss ; the rock represents an island rising independently
out of the sea. Over to the left of the
curving *karamon* (Chinese-style entry-
way), the layers of shrubbery surround a
karetaki (dry waterfall) stonework for
which the garden is well-known.

8

3. 龍源院方丈南庭
昭和　枯山水
一枝坦の名をもつ端正な庭。大海原
の白砂の中、丸い苔山が亀島、奥の屹
立した石組が蓬莱山を表している。

3. Ryōgen-in
Showa period ; dry landscape garden
Named after part of the founder's special
name—Ryoen-isshi no Ken—this garden,
Isshidan, was partially redone in 1980. In
the middle of the ocean of white sand is
a *kameshima* (tortoise island) while off to
the right stands a *tsurushima* (crane
island). The largest stonework standing
upright represents Mt. Hōrai, the mytho-
logical dwelling place of the immortal
sages in ancient China.

⑨

4．龍源院方丈北庭
室町時代　枯山水
龍吟庭と呼ばれる。力強い三尊石組
からなる須弥山形式の庭園。一面の
杉苔が大海原を表している。

4. Ryōgen-in

Muromachi period ; dry landscape garden
Circling around the hallway to the opposite side of the hall lies the famous
Ryūgintei, said to have been designed by
Soami. The *sanson iwagumi* stonework is
comprised of a centrally standing rock
with two lower "escorts." The overall
stonework depicts a waterfall flowing
into the ocean of lush spruce-moss.

5．龍源院坪庭
江戸時代　枯山水
東滴壺。方丈と庫裏の間の狭い地に
一滴の波紋から大海原を現出させる。
悠久の広がりをもつ枯淡な風趣の庭。

5. Ryōgen-in

Edo period ; dry landscape *tsubo-niwa* (small enclosed garden)
On the right at the opposite end of the entry hall lies Totekiko, an enclosed *tsuboniwa*. The waves from just one drop of water extend outward over the whole vast ocean. The simple refinement of the garden draws one's attention in a very unobtrusive way.

6．大仙院方丈東北庭
室町時代　枯山水
枯滝から流れ落ちた清流は石橋をく
ぐり、舟石を置いた大河へと続く。
大刈込が深山幽谷を表している。

6. Daisen-in
Muromachi period ; dry landscape
garden
Visualize a waterfall cascading
down the mountain and into the
valley below. From there the
white sand creates the feeling of a
river that flows under the stone
bridge winding its way to the
ocean. The emerald green of the
plants adds to the impression of
mountainous depths.

7．大仙院方丈南庭
室町時代　枯山水
東庭からの大河が南庭に至って大海
原となる。白砂敷と一対の砂盛だけ
で完成している広々とした庭。

7. Daisen-in
Muromachi period ; dry landscape garden
Here lies that vast ocean which the river
from the Eastern garden opens into. In
contrast to the detail and diversity of the
other garden, the very simplicity of this
one speaks of tranquility and transcen-
dence.

⑬

8. 高桐院方丈南庭
江戸時代　枯山水
全面の紅葉の中に一基の燈籠が寂然
と据っている。簡素ながら野趣に富
んだ庭。苔地に映る緑の夏も美しい。

8. Kōtō-in
Edo period ; dry landscape garden
The tranquility of this garden can be felt
while gazing at the single lantern surrounded by the autumn colors of the
fallen leaves as well as in winter when it
is blanketed in white. The summer green
carpet of moss equally expresses the
richness of the life of the garden.

14

9. 孤蓬庵忘筌席露地
江戸時代　枯山水
上部に四枚の明り障子を入れ、下半
分から露結の手水鉢、寄せ燈籠など
舟窓から望むかのように見せている。

9. Kohō-an
Edo period ; dry landscape garden
The four panels in the upper por-
tion of the *shoji* circumscribe
what is visible of the garden from
inside the tea room called Bosen.
Note the low height of the hand
washing basin, requiring the user
to stoop, a physical action that
carries over to the psychological
feeling of humbling oneself. Mod-
esty is an essential component of
the tea-ceremony adept. Appreciate the texture of the rocks com-
prising the stone lantern and the
glistening of the bed of black
stones surrounding it.

⑮

10. 孤篷庵書院前庭
江戸時代　枯山水
小堀遠州が晩年を送るため、郷里の
近江八景を型どって造ったといわれ
る。優しく風雅な調子の庭。

10. Kohō-an
Edo period ; dry landscape garden
Kobori Enshu designed this fine garden
late in his life, attempting to recreate the
famous "eight views of Ōmi," Ōmi being
Enshu's home province. The expansive-
ness here contrasts vividly with the more
tightly structured garden viewed previ-
ously, demonstrating the breadth and
depth of this master garden designer's
genius.

11. 芳春院方丈南庭
平成元年　枯山水
「桔梗の庭」として親しまれていた
が、近年改修された。深山より滔々と
流れ出す枯流れの美しい庭となった。

11. Hōshun-in

Heisei period ; dry landscape garden
This recently reconstructed garden
should let anyone know that the genius
of garden design in Japan is well and
flourishing and not merely a past memory. One needn't think older is necessar-
ily better. The *karetaki* stonework and
the river of white sand flow majestically
towards the ocean of our own consciousness.

12. 芳春院方丈北庭
江戸時代　楼閣山水
飽雲池に臨む二層の楼閣・呑湖閣か
ら築山へ向い、多数の石組や植栽が
続く。池中の睡蓮や燕子花が華やか。

12. Hōshun-in
Edo period; pavilion and pond
landscape garden
From the upper level of the Don-
kokaku, one has a commanding
view of the pond and *tsukiyama*
(artificial mountain) off to one
side of the building. The garden
abounds in stonework and a variety of plant life, including water
lilies and *nadeshiko*, a very delicate pink flower often symbolizing the ideal Japanese woman.

13. 聚光院方丈南庭
桃山時代　枯山水
百石の庭。積石の庭。緑深い苔庭の
生垣に平行して島を型どった石組が
配され、低く石橋が渡されている。

13. Jukō-in
Momoyama period ; dry landscape garden
The "Garden of Myriad Stones," as it is
affectionately called displays elements of
the earlier Momoyama period's penchant
for showiness in contrast to the simpler
and more traditional dry landscape gardens. A stone bridge serves to bring
together the various stonework and the
sea of moss, brilliant after an early
morning or afternoon shower.

⑲

14. 瑞峯院方丈南庭
昭和　枯山水

独坐の庭。大刈込と屹立する巨石の
蓬莱山から小島へ、砂紋は荒波を描
く。寺号「瑞峯」をテーマにしている。

14. Zuihō-in
Showa period ; dry landscape garden

Powerful waves resonate outward
from the single stone buddha sitting in meditation. Along with an
abundance of finely trimmed
hedges and large stonework mar-
bled with vertical fissures engen-
dering visions of mountain peaks
and islands, the overall composition of the garden compels us to
take time to appreciate its beauty.

15. 酬恩庵方丈東北庭
江戸時代　枯山水
深山幽谷の趣をもつ堂々たる巨石の
二段枯滝。渓谷から、苔のなか祀堂
を巡り奔流となる豪快な石組。

15. Shūon-an
Edo period ; dry landscape garden
As the years pass, the moss surrounding
this basically stonework garden serves
to accentuate the lushness bursting forth
from the double *karetaki* waterfall. It is a
pleasure to envision the peaks and val-
leys simulated by the many stoneworks
set in a variety of positions.

16. 酬恩庵方丈南庭
江戸時代　枯山水
森を背景に一休廟と桧皮葺きの虎丘
庵が見え、蘇鉄やさつきの刈込が並
ぶ。広々とした白砂が明るい庭。

16. Shūon-an
Edo period ; dry landscape garden
A finely trimmed azalea hedge serves as
a border between the garden and the
mausoleum for Sojun Ikkyu Zenji. It also
provides a curtain to enclose the deep
forests suggested in the shrubbery piled
high and set behind the ocean of white
sand—all of this visible from the *hojo*.
To see these two gardens at Shūon-an is
to appreciate the range in composition
used in dry landscape gardens.

㉒

17. 退蔵院方丈西庭
室町時代　枯山水
築山に枯滝、枯池に亀島、これに石
橋をかけ、築山の裾に蓬萊山石組を
据えている。狩野元信の作と伝える。

17. Taizō-in
Muromachi period ; dry landscape garden
The rock bridging the inner island to the
shore abounding in other magnificent
stonework is impressive. The richness of
the emerald forests of shrubbery and the
white river of gravel add to the Kano-
esque landscape. It is said that Motonobu
Kano, a famous landscape painter during
the late Muromachi early Edo periods,
lived at Taizō-in for some time.

㉓

18. 退蔵院余香苑
昭和　池泉廻遊
大刈込の深山の向うから、三段落の滝が流れ落ちる。中根金作氏作庭の刈込と清冽な水が優雅な大庭園。

18. Taizō-in
Showa period ; *chisenkaiyu* or stroll garden with pond. From a point opposite the entrance, the view of the vast green well-trimmed shrubbery bordering along the left side behind the pond of clear water delights so many who visit Taizō-in to enjoy this garden designed by Nakane Kinsaku. Flowing into the pond is a three-tiered waterfall. The shape of the vertical mountain rocks in the depth of the garden forests contrast with the lower flat river rocks in front.

㉔

19. 東海庵書院西庭
江戸時代　枯山水
大小の飛石や石組、刈込を配した苔
庭。中央奥の巨石による蓬萊三尊石
組が眼をひく。

19. Tōkai-an
Edo period ; dry landscape garden
The small and large stonework along
with shrubbery suggestive of deep forests blend well with the ocean carpet of
moss. The three large vertical rocks
introduce an element of the *shoin* or
reading hall style suggest the three holy
islands that serve as dwelling places for
Buddhist and Taoist sages. These "three
holy mountains" were located in the
Tōkai province in China from which the
temple took its name.

25

20. 東海庵中庭
江戸時代　枯山水
四方正面の狭い中庭に、大小7個の
石を直線状に繋いでいる。簡素な中
に、無限の禅的精神を表現している。

20. Tōkai-an
Edo period; dry landscape *naka-niwa* garden
The *nakaniwa* are building-enclosed gardens; this one is no exception. The theme of the unlimited being present in the infinitesimal is expressed simply but boldly by the seven rocks. In Buddhism, the number seven appears frequently symbolizing, among other things, the compassion of the buddha.

21. 桂春院書院前庭
江戸時代　枯山水
茶室・既白庵へ通じる露地庭の一角。
楓の大木、枝折戸をひかえ、苔むした
蹲踞や燈籠が佗びの精神を伝える。

21. Keishun-in
Edo period ; *rojiniwa* or tea garden
The function of the tea garden is to serve
as a transitional pathway from the busi-
ness and noise of the secular world to the
serenity of the world of tea. What a
pleasure to pause long enough to gaze at
the maple tree and lantern, feeling the
rusticity of this garden pathway while
ladling water from the moss blanketed
basin before proceeding to Kihaku-an a
tea room at the opposite end of the garden.

22. 東林院方丈庭園
江戸時代　枯山水
豊かな苔に覆われた築山に、沙羅双樹（夏椿）が白い花を降らせる。梅雨の季節に儚げな風情を見せる庭。

22. Tōrin-in
Edo period ; dry landscape garden
The vantage point from the *hojo* or abbot's quarters is a perfect one from which to take in the sal tree, symbolic of the Buddha's entry into Nirvana. The tree extends over the *tsukiyama* which itself is covered with a splendid carpet of moss. The stepping stones in the front of the garden harmonize well, creating a very natural border to the overall composition.

23. 龍安寺方丈庭園
室町時代　枯山水
白砂に15個の石を配しただけの庭
は、見る人の心に様々に映る。背景の
深い緑と油土塀が庭を引き締めている。

23. Ryōan-ji
Muromachi period ; dry landscape garden
Bordered on three sides by an earthen
wall and beyond that by a backdrop of
lush greenery, the simplicity and, at the
same time, grandeur of this garden can
be appreciated best in the early morning
—before all the other tourists arrive.
The fifteen rocks placed amidst a sea of
white sand have attracted attention from
garden designers around the world for
many many years.

24. 龍安寺鏡容池
鎌倉時代　池泉廻遊
かって「おしどり池」と呼ばれた。北
に並ぶ山々、咲き誇る桜や雪柳も艶や
かに、四季それぞれの美しさを持つ。

24. Ryōan-ji
Kamakura period ; stroll garden with pond
Walking around Oshidori Pond, views of
the delicate and seemingly snow filled
branches of the *yukiyanagi* in full bloom,
the cherry trees bursting forth in pink in
the springtime and the richness of the
surrounding hills enable one to enjoy the
environs of Ryōan-ji year round.

25. 金閣寺庭園
鎌倉時代　池泉廻遊
背後の衣笠山を借景とし、広々とし
た鏡湖池が金閣の輝きを水面に映し
出す。池には名石が多く点在する。

25. Kinkaku-ji (The Golden Pavilion)
Kamakura period ; stroll garden with pond
Through meticulous planning the
designers of this Ashikaga Yoshimitsu
patronized palace—temple, brought into
harmony the concept of the "three
depths." The golden pavilion, built in the
Sung dynasty style, served as the viewing position of the smaller rock and plant
elements in the foreground extending
outward to the pond and culminating in
the "borrowed scenery" of Mt. Kinugasa
in the background.

26. 銀閣寺庭園
室町時代　池泉廻遊
緑に囲まれた銀閣を背景に、月光を
捉えた波心を表す銀沙灘と富士の型
に白砂を盛った向月台が浮び上がる。

26. Ginkaku-ji (The Silver Pavilion)
Muromachi period; stroll garden with pond
The pavilion itself is silver in name only,
in contrast to its golden counterpart
across town. Afterall, Ashikaga Yoshimasa didn't want to upstage his
grandfather, Yoshimitsu. There are two
distinct areas to this garden : the pond,
its plants and rocks inviting memories of
by gone days in Japanese and Chinese
literature and a Mt. Fuji-style mound of
white sand that extends outward at the
base.

32

27. 南禅院方丈庭園
鎌倉時代 池泉廻遊
鬱蒼と繁る老樹を負う庭は、亀山上皇の離宮当時の面影を残す。曹源池と呼ばれ、中央に心字島がある。

27. Nanzen-in
Kamakura period; stroll garden with pond
Initially constructed by retired Emperor Kameyama to be used as his villa, the garden in Nanzen-in has survived several changes. The pond garden tends to reflect more the opulence of those who patronized Zen than of the influence of Zen aesthetics. (In the middle of the pond is a Mt. Horai stonework, a rock depicting, according to Konjaku Monogatari, a mythical dwelling place of immortal sages in China.)

28. 南禅寺方丈庭園
江戸時代　枯山水
塀に沿って東隅に六個の石と松や
楓、さつきなどの植栽が並ぶ。白砂の
空間を前景に広く残した構図をもつ。

28.Nanzen-ji
Edo period ; dry landscape garden
The moss, azalea, maple and pine all
flourishing amidst the large stonework
and bordering the ocean of white sand,
harmonize unexpectedly well with the
buildings, the roofs, and the backdrop of
the forested hillside. "Unexpectedly"
because common sense would seem to
indicate that the rocks are too large for
the plantings. Sometimes common sense
has to bow to uncommon aesthetics.

34

29. 天授庵方丈東庭
南北朝時代　枯山水
正門より本堂に至る幾何学的な石畳
が苔や深い緑と見事に調和してい
る。明治時代に改修された。

29. Tenju-an
Nambokucho or Period of the
Northern and Southern King-
doms; dry landscape and pond
garden
The border at the far end of the
garden opposite the entrance
forms one shore of the vast ocean
of white sand laid out along the
south side of the *hojo*. This border
is comprised of several large
geometrically-shaped flat stones.
From the veranda of the *hojo*
beyond the ocean rises layer upon
layer of well-trimmed "forests" of
shrubbery. The power of the tsurukame (tortoise‐crane) motif
stonework is another delight of
this garden.

30. 金地院方丈南庭
江戸時代　枯山水
白砂の庭に大曲りの手法で展開する
切石敷の飛石。深山幽谷を表す刈込
に、鶴島・亀島が力強く組まれる。

30. Konchi-in

Edo period; dry landscape and pond garden
The border at the far end of the garden
opposite the entrance forms one shore
for the vast ocean of white sand laid out
along the southside of the *hojo*. This
border is cromprised of several large
geometrically-shaped flat stones. From
the veranda of the *hojo* and beyond the
"ocean" rises layer upon layer of well-
trimmed shrubbery. The power of the
tsurukame motif of stonework is another
delight of this garden.

31．東福寺開山堂前庭
江戸時代　池泉廻遊
山の斜面を利用した築山と、参道に
沿って穿った細長い池に配した刈込
や短冊石橋が印象的な庭園。

31. Tōfuku-ji
Edo period ; stroll garden with pond
This rather elongated garden utilizes the *tsukiyama* or artificially built up mound for a mountainous effect. The narrow pond along the pathway leading to the founder's hall is crisscrossed with slender *tanzaku* shaped bridges and dotted with shrubbery, rocks and flowers. To the left side of the path is a checkerboard pattern of white sand lying before a shrubbery enclosed *tsurukame* island.

32. 東福寺方丈北庭
昭和　枯山水
正方形の切石と杉苔で市松模様が美
しく織りなされている。南庭の枯山水
の砂紋とともに斬新なデザインの庭。

32. Tōfuku-ji
Showa period; dry landscape garden
Designed by Shigemori Mirei, this
fine garden also displays a
checkerboard effect called
ichimatsu moyo comprised of
rectangularly-shaped flat stones
placed harmoniously amidst a
thick bed of spruce moss. The
pink of the azelea adds color
when in bloom in spring.

38

33. 雪舟寺方丈南庭
室町時代　枯山水
青々とした苔地に、二重基段で頭を
東に向け、背に巨石を突き立てた亀
島と、左に鶴島(昭和改修)を置く。

33. Sesshū-ji
Muromachi period ; dry landscape garden
Beyond an ocean of white sand lies a
vast forest of moss, and amidst that, a
tsurushima to the right, a *kameshima* to
the left. The brilliant green of the moss
harmonizes well with the darker green of
the trees bordering this garden. The
famous painter Sesshu is said to have
been a supporter of the temple and
designer of this garden. Today the temple bears his name.

34．天得院方丈南庭
桃山時代　枯山水
一面の杉苔の中、小振りの石が点在する閑雅な庭。桔梗が咲く梅雨時が見頃。花頭窓から見る西庭も美しい。

34. Tentoku-in
Momoyama period ; dry landscape garden
During the rainy season the Chinese bellflower is at its best, further highlighting the brilliance of the spruce moss. Here and there are several rocks carefully laid out more than worthy of taking a few minutes to ponder over. Tentoku-in is a *tatchū* (sub-temple) of Tōfuku-ji.

40

35. 円徳院方丈北庭
桃山時代　池泉廻遊（涸）
鬱蒼と繁る木立のなか、枯滝が流れ
出し、苔むした枯池に豪壮な鶴亀島
を配する。巨大な石橋が目をひく。

35. Entoku-in
Momoyama period; dry landscape garden
There may not actually be any water
flowing down the rock waterfall nor
under the bridge, but the ocean of emerald green moss can easily deceive the
eyes into *seeing* it quite differently. Other
fine stonework including the *tsurukame*
motif and the brilliant red of the maples
in fall will leave contrasting memories of
this garden, memories of its tranquility
as well as of its dynamic vigor.

36. 高台寺庭園
江戸時代　池泉廻遊
開山堂を中心にした観月台のある橋
廊のかかる庭。山腹にある傘亭・時
雨亭の建築も見るべきものがある。

36. Kōdai-ji
Edo period ; stroll garden with pond
The pond, divided into an eastern and
western area by a bridge called *Rosenro*
or "Tower Boat Way," contains a *tsurushima* or crane island on one side with a
kameshima or tortoise island on the
other. Rosenro has a roofed-in moon
viewing platform. Historically, Kōdai-ji
has been a *tatchū* of Kennin-ji.

37. 天龍寺庭園
鎌倉時代　池泉廻遊・観賞
龍門瀑と呼ばれる滝組の前に、三枚
の自然石の石橋が組まれている。付
近の石島群と共に池泉の眼目をなす。

37. Tenryū-ji
Kamakura period; stroll garden with pond
This garden employs the principle of the
"three depth," foreground, middle-
ground, background, and contains several large rocks. One of them, *Ryūmonba-
ku* or Dragon Gate Falls, is a large
powerful stone of the *karetaki* or dry
waterfall type. It is wellknown for the
large bridge supported by two other
natural rocks. The garden is memorable,
in rain, shine, or snow.

38. 天龍寺庭園
鎌倉時代　池泉廻遊・観賞
曹源池を囲む亀山、その上からかぶ
さる嵐山、洲浜の曲線、豪放な滝組、
全てが庭園に渾然と調和している。

38. Tenryū-ji
Kamakura period ; stroll garden with pond
With the hills of Arashiyama for *shakkei*
or "borrowed scenery," Sogenchi Pond
gleams and glistens in the sunlight after
a rather heavy snowfall. Together with
the grand *karetaki* stonework and the
island jutting out from the side, the
whole composition blends quite harmoniously. The view from the veranda is as
lovely as from any other spot.

39. 等持院方丈北庭
江戸時代　池泉廻遊
書院より眺める芙蓉池庭園。北に築
山を設け草庵風茶席の清漣亭を置く。
幾重にも重なる刈込は見事である。

39. Tōji-in
Edo period ; stroll garden with pond
The stillness of a winter morning snow
lightly covering the shrubbery and stonework can all be taken in from the
veranda of the *shoin* or reading room.
Off to the side is a *tsukiyama* where the
tea hut Seirentei is located. The illusion
of deep forests has been creatively
designed with the use of abundant shrubbery.

40. 等持院方丈南庭
昭和　枯山水
左右の隅に刈込と石を配し、前面は
白砂で広がりをみせる。紅葉の頃と
雪景色がとりわけ美しい。

40. Tōji-in
Showa period ; dry landscape garden
This garden on the south side of the *hojo*
consists of a vast area of white sand
bordered on either side by rocks and
shrubbery. Appreciate the brilliant reds
and yellows of the maples in late fall or
an occasional snowscape in winter ; both
are particularly lovely.

41. 西芳寺池泉庭園
鎌倉時代　池泉廻遊
苔寺。黄金池を中心とした庭は豊か
な苔に覆われ、汀のなだらかな曲線
は大和絵的な美しさを感じさせる。

41. Saihō-ji
Kamakura period; stroll garden with pond
Known more familiarly as Kokedera or
the "Moss Temple," Saihō-ji was reconstructed by Musō Soseki who believed
that gardens were an essential setting for
meditation. Ogonchi Pond takes the
shape of the Chinese character for heart/
mind and is bordered on all sides by
many varieties of moss. There are undoubtedly few gardens anywhere that
are as ideal for strolling through as this
one.

42. 西芳寺枯山水庭園
鎌倉時代　枯山水
石までも苔に染まった三段の堅牢な
枯滝石組。上二段は力強く、下一段
は軽く流した構成が取られている。

42. Saihō-ji
Kamakura period ; dry landscape garden
Moving along the path and upward, your
footsteps will lead you to one of the
earliest examples of the dry landscape
garden. The combination of horizontal
and vertical stonework suggestive of a
multi-tiered waterfall is as lush and
animated as the pond area but without
the actual presence of the water element.

48

43. 西芳寺枯山水庭園
鎌倉時代　枯山水
洪隠山の山腹、開山堂指東庵付近の
苔庭。この近くには、夢窓国師が座禅
を組んだといわれる座禅石がある。

43. Saihō-ji
Kamakura period ; dry landscape garden
This upper area is part of the dry landscape garden. Near the *kaisandō*
(founder's hall) is a large flat rock on
which Musō Soseki, designer of the garden, is said to have meditated while looking over the garden. Most likely these
ancient sitters propped themselves up a
bit with a straw mat or cushion to enable
them to sit for longer periods of time.

44．地蔵院方丈前庭
室町時代　枯山水
椿の花降る苔地に、十六羅漢の修行
の姿を表した石が点在する。「竹の寺」
の名の如く山へと続く竹林が見える。

44. Jizō-in
Muromachi period ; dry landscape garden
Jizō-in takes its name from the Buddhist
bodhisattva, Jizō, the guardian deity of
children. In the garden sixteen arhats are
scattered about, ascetics who were disci-
ples of the Buddha. The camelias in
spring are lovely and the bamboo grove
surrounding the temple adds serenity to
the overall atmosphere.

45．正伝寺方丈東庭
江戸時代　枯山水
白砂敷を白い築地塀で囲い、石を使
わず、刈込で七五三の石組を表して
いる。比叡山を借景とする庭園。

45. Shōden-ji
Edo period ; dry landscape garden
From the veranda of the *hojo*, enjoy the
white of the ocean of sand and the wall
that comprises its border which serves to
accentuate the mounds of azalea laid out
in the seven-five-three combination. Just
beyond the wall lies a thick green forest
and the path that leads up to the temple
entrance. Finally, beyond that, rises Mt.
Hiei, the ultimate in "borrowed scenery."
The charm of Shoden-ji is its rusticity.

46. 金福寺庭園
江戸時代　枯山水
高台の三段刈込の上に、芭蕉が寓居
したという草庵の屋根が見える。つ
つじの大刈込が白砂にかぶさる。

46. Konpuku-ji
Edo period ; dry landscape garden
Along the path stoneway, the azalea and
other shrubbery rise in three tiers and in
the distance can be seen the roof of Soan,
the hut where the great haiku poet
Matsuo Basho is said to have stayed
when visiting Kyoto. Off to the left is an
ocean of white sand that extends up to
the edge of the azalea.

47. 詩仙堂庭園
江戸時代　枯山水
書院から望む半球形のさつきの大刈
込と、白砂に白山茶花の古木が床し
い庭園。ししおどし（添水）も名高い。

47. Shisen-dō
Edo period ; dry landscape garden
This landscape garden utilizes the rug-
ged hillside on which it is located. The
huge carefully trimmed azalea bushes
blossoming forth in various colors in the
spring show one face of the garden. In
the autumn their subdued green serves as
a perfect base for enjoying the red and
gold of the maples. The hydrangea, the
irises and *sazanqua* in their respective
seasons add further color.

ZEN GARDENS TEXT

by Tom Wright

Dedication

I would like to dedicate this book to Evelyn Wright, a Christian bodhisattva if there ever was one.

Ⅰ The Spirit of Zen

Picking up a newspaper these days, hardly a day goes by when we don't read about some drive-by shooting, or a deranged murderer, or perhaps the anti-Semitic effacing of gravestones or the ordering of the death penalty for a writer whose ideas (may or may not) conflict with the religious norms of his country's religion. On a mass scale, we read about the movement of whole societies against other societies for material gains (that are rarely ever, however, couched in language other than for "justice," "righteousness," or "God.")

Seeing the enormous destruction of natural disasters should be enough to cause us to lend a helping hand to our neighbors, regardless of religious beliefs, color of skin, differences of language or culture, and in fact, we do see that, too. But it seems to me that all too quickly we forget that there is only one earth and one humanity and that we ourselves make the best or worst of our world.

It is in this context that I began my own inward exploration of who I really am and what this world we live in is. After some twenty years of practicing zazen and studying various Buddhist and Christian scriptures under the direction of my teacher, Uchiyama Kôshô Rôshi, I can say the only conclusion I have come to is that I shall keep asking these questions of who I am and what this world is to the end of my days. One might think that after twenty years of practicing and studying Zen, I should surely have reached some sort of solution by now; the fact is, I haven't.

Actually, what seems to be more the case is that

the longer I do zazen —— though perhaps this is as it should be —— the more I become aware of the enormity of my own ignorance; ignorance not so much in terms of a lack of knowledge of things or of natural phenomena, though that, of course, is true too, but of the coarseness or lack of regard for the quality of my day to day life and of the people around me. It would not be a healthy thing to just brood about such matters —— brooding very often is just a disguise for escape. On the other hand, I think for people to act and be in the world and working in our society in a vigorous and vital way we need to more carefully reflect on our actions and allow those reflections to guide us to a greater awareness of what we are doing. At the same time, I believe that our reflections serve the function of motivating us to act in the most appropriate way.

Sawaki Kôdô Rôshi, the former abbott of Antai-ji and teacher of Uchiyama Rôshi, once said, "To be pulled and dragged around by zazen —— ahh, what a wonderful life!" I understand his words in this way; that selfish aspect of my character or consciousness is always and only looking after itself, but when I sit down and do zazen, that selfish aspect obviously also sits with me. And when those naturally selfish reflections of my past actions arise in my head when I'm sitting, even though I just sit there and let them come and go, they somehow seem to have a power of their own to let me know how foolish I have been.

Perhaps it seems that I'm implying that gradually, as we reflect on ourselves, we become "better" people, but that is not the case. It is not so because as long as we are living human beings, our selfish or protective aspect is not simply going to disappear. In other words, the kind of reflection I have been talking about is not a one time thing, but must be an on-going activity.

What seems to me far more important than having some half-baked *kensho* or *satori* experience of the variety we read so frequently about in books on Zen is to realize that these questions of who we are or what the world is must remain open questions. That is, once we come to some realization or conclusion about our self-identity, then we have closed off the possibility of probing further and deeper into the questions.

In many *teisho* or lectures on Buddhist scriptures, Uchiyama Rôshi used the expression *deau tokoro waga seimei* —— "whatever we encounter is our life."

I can't think of a more appropriate expression to describe the spirit of Zen than this expression. In our day to day lives we encounter many people and situation, some of them are pleasant, even enjoyable or exciting, others might make us sad or angry. Still others we prefer to put out of our minds and refuse to think about them. This phenomenon is just a matter of course and something that occurs to all human beings —— Zen adepts included. What is surprising about this, however, is how easily we allow ourselves to be pulled around by the heat of our emotions or tied up in knots by the entanglements of our thoughts, ideas, and opinions. We can see this most clearly when observing others. However, it becomes more difficult when we try to look "objectively" at ourselves.

What occurs when zazen becomes the central pillar of our lives is that we are enabled to exerience again and again in our sitting that what is painful or pleasant is nothing more than that. And that it is not necessary to be constantly pulled or pushed around by one or the other. Pain is just pain, pleasure is just pleasure. Without trying to escape from the one or chase after the other we have to simply encounter whatever it is that is before us. This is what a Buddhist would call a bodhisattva, or in Uchiyama Rôshi's words, "a true adult."

In our darkest hour, it may be only natural to call out to some Great Power outside of ourselves to help us through the day. The Moslem calls out to Allah and God, the Christian prays to Jesus Christ for help, the Jew appeals to Yahweh. What does the Buddhist do?

Whithin Buddhism, there are two main streams of thought. The one stream is to appeal to Amida Buddha, popularly thought to be living in the Western Paradise and who will come and help us in our hour of need. Generally speaking, this stream can be referred to as the stream of Other Power, that is, Amida Buddha is a power that comes to us from outside of ourselves.

The other stream of Buddhism is Zen which is popularly referred to as the stream of "Self Power." Traditionally, Zen thinkers, similarly to the atheistic existentialists like Sartre or Camus, have said that to depend on some "outside" power is nonsense and an escape from taking individual responsibility for one's life. On the other hand, the Other Power proponents in Buddhism retorted that to speak of Self Power is the ultimate in human arrogance and egotism. For Buddhist scholars this seeming dilemma provides a base for writing tomes defending one stream or the other. For the Buddhist practitioner, however, to speak of Buddhism in terms of Other Power or Self Power poses no problem whatever. There is no problem because whatever the reality of Other Power (Amida Buddha) or Self Power is, it exists or operates before we can put any sort of label on it. This will come out again later on when I talk about the importance of seeing the gardens in this book for what they are, prior to sticking the label of Zen on them.

By talking abut "Other Power" and "Self Power" I'm afraid I have strayed a little from my topic of the Zen spirit, but I feel it is necessary for readers to be able to put Zen in a context within the overall tapestry of Buddhism before discussing the particulars of the spirit and practice of it.

Zen is Zazen

Any discussion of Zen that excludes zazen would only be a discussion in abstraction, it is virtually useless. Readers should understand that for the Zen Buddhist, talk about Zen means talking about zazen, or sitting Zen. I avoid using the word "Zen meditation" here as the English word meditation has its own connotations for most Westerners. Normally, meditating implies meditating on some thing or more simply, thinking deeply about something. The practice of zazen whereby the sitter concentrates on some rationally unsolvable problem is called *kôan* Zen. A *kôan* is a terse statement or question that the sitter concentrates on during zazen (actually, throughout the whole day). *Kôan* Zen is the type of zazen practiced in the Rinzai school of Zen of which all the temples in this book (except **Shisen-dô**) are affiliated. It is, in a sense, a type of "meditation."

The type of themeless zazen advocated by Eihei Dôgen Zenji (1200–1253), founder of the Sôtô School of Zen, is called *shikantaza,* meaning just sitting. In other words, when the sitter sits down to do zazen, he or she just sits without trying to conjure up some visualization of the Buddha or work on solving some riddle.

Of course, when practicing *shikantaza,* since there is no problem, no theme, no object of visualization, it would be a very simple matter to just face the wall and go to the movies —— the "movies" being the images that arise in one's mind. Therefore, my advice to newcomers to zazen is not to suppress, not to reject, and not to chase after. Or, as Uchiyama Rôshi often said, "Open the hand of thought."

When we sit zazen, anything can and usually does arise in our head; a childhood experience we want to suppress, an unpleasant experience of being criticized by someone, and wanting to reject the criticism, or thoughts of all the nice things we'd like to buy with our next paycheck or about how close to enlightenment we must be because of our good zazen. Despite or because of the fact that we are just sitting facing the wall, we feel uncomfortable and seek to entertain ourselves by forming pleasant thoughts to think about. This wouldn't be so bad if only pleasant thoughts formed, but rarely is that ever the case. Very often, even when we're not sitting zazen, thoughts form *somewhere* despite our intention to reject or suppress them —— thoughts of the demise of a loved one (or, heaven forbid, our own death!), or our seeming loneliness, or the lack of a sense of meaning or worth in our lives.

When these thoughts continue to come up during one period of sitting or over a period of several sittings, or over a period of twenty or thirty years, we begin to become suspicious of them (even the horrible or frightening ones) and we begin to settle down and not be so pulled around by them. And living a life of just sitting deeper and deeper into ourselves without being carried away by our thoughts and emotions is living a life based on zazen. The more we practice a zazen of just letting come up whatever comes up and letting it go away, the more we realize that our thoughts are but a mirror of whatever it is that is foremost in our lives at any one time. It isn't that after sitting for many years fewer and fewer thoughts arise until we enter a state of thoughtlessness. Living

thoughtlessly is a large part of the problem of our busy frenetic society today! It is in letting the thoughts that arise in our minds come and go as if looking into a mirror but without getting carried away by them (i. e , by trying to suppress, or reject or attach to them), that the life force that runs through each and every one of us and everything around us straightens out our lives naturally, so that we are able to give full play to whatever the encounter before us calls for.

There is an expression in Zen that goes, *munen musô* —— no thought, no form. That is, it is popularly believed that if a person sits zazen hard enough and for a long enough time, then one day he or she will arrive at a state of *munen musô* —— no thought, no form —— equivalent to *satori* or enlightenment. To be sure, there are times when one sits zazen that very few or even no particular thoughts arise, but such a psychological state should never be confused with Enlightenment. If a state of no thought, no form is the ideally "enlightened" state, then the rock out in the garden is far more enlightened that I am since it has no thought!

The expression, *munen musô,* very simply put, means giving no thought to "what's in it for me?" It means not being so tied up by conventional forms that we become unable to function. For example, to be so puffed up with pride over our position as top executive in the company that we literally lose our sight towards helping others around us either in the company or in our community at large. This is also the sense of the bodhisattva vow to save all sentient beings before trying to save oneself.

In Dôgen Zenji's "Tenzo Kyôkun" (Instructions to the Cook) , Dôgen writes of the attitude of the tenzo or cook. He says that the attitude of the cook must be the same as the attitude of the abbot. And what is that attitude?

"···The three aspects of this attitude are to see that working for the benefit of others benefits oneself, to understand that through making every effort for the prosperity of the community one revitalizes one's own character, and to know that endeavoring to succeed and to surpass the patriarchs of past generations means to learn from their lives and to value their examples. "

In a similar context Dôgen writes of what he calls "parental mind, "

"···A parent, irrespective of poverty or difficult circumstances, loves and raises a child with care. How deep is love like this? Only a parent can understand it. A parent protects the children from the cold and shades them from the hot sun with no concern for his or her own personal welfare. Only a person in whom this mind has arisen can understand it, and only one in whom this attitude has become second nature can fully manifest it. This is the attitude in being a parent." (Refining Your Life, Kôshô Uchiyama, Weatherhill, 1983, pp.15-17)

II Buddhism arrives in Japan

Buddhism first came to Japan via Korea and China some time during the sixth century. For several tens of years there was a struggle between whose deities were more powerful, the local Shinto ones or the Buddhist ones. In practical terms, the struggle was of a political nature between the various clans surrounding the Imperial Court. Finally, it was the civilizing and cultural accouterments (a written language brought by calligraphers as well as pottery and textile making brought by different artisans) that accompanied the religion and the strong personality of Prince Shotoku (574-622) that helped to unify the so-called progressive factions within the society enabling Buddhism to enter and to lay its roots in Japan. This early Buddhism was highly esoteric, ritualistic and ceremonial in its structure. Despite its message of universal equality, in practice, it belonged to the ruling elite. Vast numbers of the common people who became Buddhists undoubtedly did so simply because the rulers of their clan had done so. A somewhat dated but quite readable volume on the history of Buddhism in Japan is Masaharu Anesaki's History of Japanese Religion.

III The Second wave — Pure Land and Zen

As Buddhism became more and more entrenched in Japan, its forms became increasingly ritualistic and its political strength more of a threat to the rulers. A kind of simple peitism developed among the common people and the effete aristocracy that involved a recitation of the *nembutsu*. It was believed that by reciting this short three-word prayer "Namu Amida Butsu," ([I take] refuge [in] Amida Buddha) that one would be reborn in the Pure Land called Jôdo. Hence, the name of the school became to be called Jôdo-shû or Pure Land Buddhism. Paralleling a resurgence of this school which was led by Shinran Shonin and subsequently became known as the New Pure Land School (Jôdo Shinshû) was another movement, Zen. Although Zen was introduced into Japan around the 10th century, it never made any major advances until Myôan Eisai (1141-1215) and Eihei Dôgen (1200- 1254) emphasized zazen more than any earlier Buddhist figure. It is from these two men that the Rinzai and Sôtô schools of Zen evolved. By the 13th century, the older schools of Buddhism had declined and the Buddhism found in the monasteries in Sung dynasty China was basically Zen Buddhism. As the doors between China and Japan were opening again and trade between the two countries increased, the Kamakura Shogunate invited eminent priests to Japan to teach Buddhism and Chinese arts and letters. By and large, the priests who arrived and became the teachers of both Buddhism and Chinese literature were Zen priests. In contrast to the older schools of Buddhism which over the centuries had acquired vast wealth in the form of land, and had even built up powerful military contingents called *sôhei* or soldier monks, the "new" Zen school was totally dependent on the patronage of the Kamakura *bakufu* led by the Hojo line, and later by the Ashikaga family and the emperors.

Besides inviting eminent Chinese priests to come to Japan to teach Zen, Japanese priests were also sent to China to study Zen and Chinese culture. Myôan Eisai (or, sometimes Yôsai) is credited with introducing Rinzai Zen into Japan, although a great deal of credit should also go to Enni Ben'en (1202-1280) as well as Musô Soseki (1275-1351). Following the threat of Mongol invasions of Japan in mid-thirteenth century, Musô was apparently rather upset that so much time was being devoted to *kitô*, prayers and invocations for survival of the country resulting in a reduction in time spent sitting zazen. With the support of the Hojo Shogunate, Musô worked to propagate this new teaching and establish Zen as an institution. Another pillar in the establishment of Zen in Japan was Eihei Dôgen. After studying Tendai Buddhism on Mt. Hiei, Dôgen practiced Rinzai Zen under Eisai's chief disciple, Myôzen Butsuju (1184-1225) at **Kennin-ji.** Later the two of them visited China where Myôzen died. Dôgen returned to Japan, however, and eventually established the Sôtô school of Zen at **Eihei-ji** in present day Fukui Prefecture, away from the hustle and bustle of metropolitan life and from the power politics and intrigues that were taking place at the time within the Imperial family itself and between the Imperial family and the Kamakura shogunate. That is why even today the dominant Zen school found in Kyoto is the Rinzai school, of which all the temples in this book belong (except for **Shisen-dô**) .

IV The Gozan System

During the Kamakura period when the Hôjô family line was in power, and during the following Muromachi period when political power returned to Kyoto and rested in the hands of the Ashikaga, the Zen school grew and flourished within the warrior class and found favor with several emperors as well. Without the patronage of successive shoguns and emperors, we would undoubtedly not be able to admire the many fine gardens that survive in Kyoto today.

The reasons for shogunal and imperial support of Zen are complex and would require volumes of explanation. Two major reasons, one external and one internal, are that it was Zen that carried the greatest weight and was most widespread when Japan and China reopened their doors to one another and, the Kamakura shogunate was in the market for a force (intellectual and cultural) that might come in handy in offsetting the tremendous wealth and power of the older Buddhist schools.

The outcome was the establishment of the *gozan* or "five mountains" system imported from China and adapted to the Japanese situation. During the earlier Tang dynasty (618-906) in China, as Zen was practiced and thrived mostly in the rural mountainous areas and Zen temples were mountain temples, the tradition of attaching the word "mountain" to the name of the temple survived long after many monasteries began to be located in metropolitan areas. In fact, many of the early Zen masters took their names from the mountain they lived on, somewhat like referring to them as Master Pikes Peak or Master

Blanc. So despite the fact that almost all of the temples and sub-temples in this book are located within flat metropolitan Kyoto, they all contain "mountain" in their official names. More specifically, the *gozan* or "five mountains" are **Nanzen-ji, Tenryû-ji, Tôfuku-ji, Kennin- ji,** and **Shôkoku-ji. Daitoku-ji** was designated a *gozan* of the first rank when Godaigo was Emperor (1334-1336), but asked to be exempted from the system quite early on in order to preserve its independence. **Myôshin-ji** was even more of a maverick and never was a part of the *gozan* system. A most fascinating and detailed account of the various aspects of the *gozan* system available in English is Martin Collcutt's Five Mountains —— The Rinzai Zen Monastic Institution in Medieval Japan.

Although the *gozan* system refers to the Rinzai Zen monastic institution, there can be little doubt that it was not in the control of the resident priests and monks. Looking back at those who served in the administration of that system, it is difficult to say whether they were monastic-bureaucrats or bureaucratic-priests. What is unambiguous, however, is that their loyalties and service served the shogunate government and, the function of the system was to keep this "new" Buddhist school under shogunate control, not allowing it to grow in material wealth and military power in the way the older Buddhist schools had done on Mt.Hiei and Mt.Kôya.

Just what controls over monastic affairs did the *soroku* or bureaucratic office for carrying out *gozan* affairs have? To be sure, prior to its establishment, Zen monasteries had their own regulations governing the life of the monastery. Such things as how to eat, how to behave, when to do zazen and for how long, etc. were all regulated. However, as I mentioned briefly, when Zen was introduced and spread throughout the country during the Kamakura period, the monasteries had little wealth or land of their own. The funds to cover the construction of the buildings and to maintain them came directly from the *bakufu* or possibly from some wealthy samurai, or, funds or land were donated by the imperial family. These secular "gifts" were not free. The cost to the monasteries was independence over their affairs. A few areas that were under the control of the *bakufu* were; "1, prodigality, 2, wandering, 3, contact with women, 4,novices and postulants, 5, total number of inhabitants, 6, weapons, 7,abbots, 8, the two ranks of officers, 9, economic affairs, 10, religious matters". (Colcutt, p.166). It appears that, more than anything else, the *soroku* was concerned with maintaining control over the economic affairs of the monasteries. The *bakufu's* hand in religious matters doesn't seem to have been very large until the extravagances within the monasteries began to overly influence the daily life of the residents later on in the Muromachi period.

V Temples and Tatchû (sub-temples)

When we first hear the name of one of these famous temples such as **Daitoku-ji** or **Tôfuku-ji**, we probably imagine some sort of large temple building where many monks are walking around in robes bowing to one another. In actuality, the name **Daitoku-ji**, for example, refers to an entire temple complex consisting of the **Daitoku-ji** *sôdô* (monks' hall and grounds) in addition to twenty-three *tatchû* (sub-temples) scattered around the grounds. And, although there might be twenty or thirty monks living full-time within the *sôdô* itself, there is usually only one or two priests, possibly with their families, living at any one time in a sub-temple.

Looking briefly at the sub-temples that will appear in this book, besides the **Daitoku-ji** *sôdô* and accompanying buildings (founded, 1319) and within the **Daitoku-ji** grounds are **Ryôgen-in** (founded, 1504), **Daisen-in** (1509), **Kôtô-in** (1603), **Kohô-an** (1621), **Hôshun-in** (1608), **Jukô-in** (1582) and **Zuihô-in** (1541). **Shûon-an** is a *matsu-ji* (branch temple) belonging to **Daitoku-ji**, but it is not located within the **Daitoku-ji** precincts. It is to be found a few miles south of the city where, it is said, Ikkyu Zenji spent some time.

"Deprived of its status as an official monastery, and thus of Ashikaga patronage, **Daitoku-ji** eventually found three new sources of economic support, the merchant community of the city of Sakai, the emerging Warring States barons —— *sengoku daimyo,* and, third, the tea masters (*chajin*), linked- verse masters (*rengashi*), noh actors, and other arbiters of contemporary culture who were familiar with Zen monks, consorted with merchants, and served powerful

daimyo." (Five Mountains, Collcutt, pp125-126)

Among the 15 branches of the Rinzai school of Zen, **Myôsin-ji** is the largest with over 40 *tatchû* on the grounds and over 3,500 *matsu-ji* throughout Japan. **Myôshin-ji** was established with the patronage of Emperor Hanazono (1297-1348), in 1337. It was never included among the *gozan* temples undoubtedly for political reasons, but also due to its more frugal and severe regimen. Hanazono invited Kanzan Egen to be its founder. Kanzan had studied and practiced under Shuho Myocho, the founder of **Daitoku-ji**. **Taizô-in** (founded 1404), **Tôkai-an** (1484), **Keishun-in** (1598) and **Tôrin-in** (1556) are just four of the *tatchû* that were established over the centuries. **Taizô-in**, **Tôkai-an**, and **Tôrin-in** were founded during the Muromachi period while **Keishun-in** was founded by Suian Sokoku and patronized first by Tsuda Hidenori and later by Ishikawa Sadamasa, about the time Toyotomi Hideyoshi took control of the country.

Ryôan-ji (founded, 1499) formerly served as the grounds of a Fujiwara nobleman. The dry landscape garden here is comprised solely of the fifteen rocks and sea of white sand. It is probably the most photographed garden of its kind in Japan.

Shôkoku-ji (founded, 1382), **Nanzen-ji**, **Tôfuku-ji**, **Kennin-ji** and **Tenryû-ji** comprise the *gozan* or "Five Mountains." Though not located on the grounds of **Shôkoku-ji**, both **Kinkaku-ji** and **Ginkaku-ji** (the Gold and Silver Pavilions, respectively) are affiliated with the **Shôkoku-ji** branch of the Rinzai school. Both received the patronage of the Ashikaga Shogunate, the former was the retired villa-monastery of Ashikaga Yoshimitsu (1358-1409) while the latter served first as the retirement villa for the sixth Ashikaga shôgun and grandson of Yoshimitsu, Yoshimasa.

Nanzen-ji was founded in 1290 and served originally as the detached palace of Emperor Kameyama (1249-1305) who had it converted into a Zen temple at that time. **Nanzen-in**, a sub-temple of **Nanzen-ji** was the retirement villa for the emperor when he retired in 1274, and later became a part of the **Nanzen-ji** complex. The garden here, though originally constructed during the Kamakura period, was reconstructed several times. M. Treib and R. Herman in A Guide to the Gardens in Kyoto suggest that placing it in the early Edo period would be more accurate. **Tenju-an** was built as a *tatchû* in memory of Daimyoin Kokushi. The original garden was redesigned as a stroll garden in 1905. **Konchi-in** served as the *sôroku*, an office under the control of the *bakufu* and technically in charge of "···the appointment and promotion of abbots and monastic officers, collection of fees, ranking of monasteries, granting of monastic domain, and maintenance of standards of monastic life, "(Five Mountains, p.122) during the seventeenth century." I say "technically" because in reality, the office by that time had lost whatever power it had once held.

Tôfuku-ji was founded in 1236 (although it took ten years to finish construction of the buildings) by Enni Ben'en and was supported by the regent, Kujo Michiie. It is said that Michiie wanted to create a structure in Kyoto that would surpass any of the monasteries of the older Buddhist schools in Nara.

Sesshû-ji, or Funda-in as it is more formally known, was founded by Soan Jojin about 1321 and

backed by Uchitsune Ichijô. This sub-temple of **Tôfuku-ji** was the *bodai-ji* (family temple) for the Ichijô family. The temple suffered over time from fire and neglect, but thanks to Shigemori Mirei in 1959 and Nakane Kinsaku, who made extensive repairs on the garden in 1957, the grounds today have been completely renovated. **Tentoku-in**, also a sub-temple of **Tôfuku-ji**, displays a dry landscape garden influenced by the earlier flamboyant Momoyama period.

Regarding **Kôdai-ji** and **Entoku-in**, there are a variety of histories available and one has to choose whose story, his story or hers, to believe. The ravages of disasters —— human and natural —— and time, make sketching a history just that-an approximate sketch. **Kôdai-ji** and **Entoku-in** are sub-temples connected to **Kennin-ji**, one of the earliest built Zen temples. In all probability **Kôdai-ji** was established around 1605 by Toyotomi Hideyoshi's wife in commemoration of her late husband. **Entoku-in** is a reconstruction of a building and garden formerly located in Fushimi Castle, Hideyoshi's headquarters. The temple was brought to its present site and presented to the nephew (or brother, according to other sources) of Hideyoshi's wife. **Entoku-in** derives its name from the Buddhist name taken by the brother, (or was it the nephew?) Kinoshita Toshifumi, at his ordination —— Entokuin.

After the death of Emperor Godaigo, his successor, Emperor Kogon, was prevailed upon by Ashikaga Takauji and his younger brother, Tadayoshi, to build a memorial for the former emperor. The result was **Tenryû-ji**. Originally, the temple had been the detached palace of Kogon who issued orders to have it converted into a Zen monastery with Musô Soseki as its founder. Construction of the temple was financed through taxes collected from various *shôen* or landed estates that existed throughout the country. Not enough funds, however, necessitated the sending of a trade mission to China which appears to have been highly profitable, according to Professor Collcutt's research reported in <u>Five Mountains</u>.

Musô Soseki divided his time between **Tenryû-ji**, **Rinsen-ji** (not in this book) and **Saihô-ji** which is a converted Pure Land school temple. Musô is sometimes credited with designing the paradise garden there, but that is highly unlikely. What he probably did was renovate a garden that had been in disrepair and add his own touches. It will be noted that the founding dates for **Tenryû-ji** and **Saihô-ji** (as a Zen monastery) are approximately the same. The dismantling and reconstruction of **Tôji-in** at its present site followed about two years later. It served as the *bodai-ji* for the Ashikaga line. It was a high ranking *jissatsu* temple (one rank under a *gozan* temple). It's possible but doubtful that Musô Soseki had a hand in the garden's design. In any event, the fragrance of the *mokusei* (sweet osmanthus) in the autumn is especially delightful.

While **Saihô-ji** is better known as the Moss Temple, **Jizô-in** may be more familiar to Japanese as the Bamboo Temple. **Jizô-in** was founded in 1367 by Sokyo Zenji and built by Hosokawa Yoriyuki, a governor-general of the Ashikaga. He himself was a Fujiwara whose ancestors played such a powerful role earlier in Japanese history.

Shôden-ji was founded in 1268 by a Chinese emigre monk, Gottan, who was fleeing the Mongol invasion in China. It was put to the torch by the soldier-monks or *sôhei* of **Enryaku-ji** and reconstructed at its present site in 1282. The story goes that when Gottan fled to Japan and tried to enter **Kenchô-ji** in Kamakura, he received the scowls of the monks there because he refused to pay obeisance to the statue of the bodhisattva, Jizô, enshrined there. He is reported to have said. "I'm a fully enlightened buddha. It would be more appropriate for that bodhisattva to pay respect to me." (<u>Miyako no Niwa</u>, Koma Toshio, Yamazaki, 1980, p.94) Now there was a man with no lack of self-confidence···**Konpuku-ji**, also allied to **Nanzen-ji**, was favored by the monk-artist Sesshu spoken of earlier, and also by the famous haiku poet, Matsuo Basho. Buson, a contemporary of Basho, is said to have renovated Basho-an.

Shisen-dô, literally, the "Temple of Poet Sages," was the hermitage of Ishikawa Jozan, a former samurai and poet. There is one small room that contains the portraits of 36 famous Chinese poets. These are said to have been painted by Kano Tanyu. Sitting on the veranda one can occasionally hear the sharp crack of the *sôzu*, a device utilizing bamboo and water that functions to chase away deer. (You'll have to imagine the deer in our age, however)

Volumes more could be said about each of these temples and their respective gardens, but now it's time to just enjoy them for what they are. Even after reading my all too brief description, I think the reader can as least get a hint that there is no such thing as a "pure" Zen temple. If the temples and these gardens had not had the political backing and financial support of the Hôjô and Ashikaga shogunate governments, as well as that of successive emperors, they would not be in existence today. To be sure, there have been many Zen monks down through the ages in Japan (most of whose names shall never be known) who practiced zazen quietly and stayed away from the clamor and intrigues of Zen as an economic and political force in Japan. Should all these temples and gardens built with enormous sums of money and labor extracted from the people for the benefit of the few, be dismissed outright as merely the playthings of the aristocracy and remnants of decadence? There are some people who feel that way, although I think that such judgements may be a bit too simplistic. The answer is for you to decide.

Many young Americans and Europeans have come to Japan over the years seeking the "pure" Zen experience —— whatever that is. Today most people looking into Zen come here having read and studied more on the subject than those of years past. Besides the large Zen centers in California or New York or Paris, many fine small centers such as those in rural Massachusetts as well as in America's heartland are popping up all the time. Just how these centers will grow and become a part of the mainstream of Western cultural and religious life remains to be seen. To be sure, it will take a lot more than the simple imitation of Sung dynasty customs or clothing to change peoples' values towards the life of all humanity and our environment. For me, the "garden" that needs the greatest work on is the garden of our very own lives and the gardener is our zazen.

VI A Few Words on Japanese Gardens

I have devoted most of this writing to the spirit of Zen and tried to place it in an historical context alongside the other, earlier schools of Buddhism. I've discussed briefly the *gozan* system of ranking temples and made a few comments about the specific temples whose gardens appear in these photographs of Katsuhiko Mizuno. It was never intended that this book be anything other than an introduction to the temples and gardens of Kyoto, and to place them in a perspective for visitors to Kyoto. For those wishing to go further into the background of Zen in Japan and Zen gardens, I have provided a brief list at the end of this book for that purpose. Still, I would like to conclude by taking a brief look at a few of the fundamental ideas that go into Japanese gardens and how these ideas have been passed down through the ages, not from the view of the specialist (which I am not) but simply as a sort of distillation of what I have read and felt about the gardens here.

The tradition of garden design in Japan has been passed down in various ways; through esoteric texts such as Sakuteiki (Notes on Garden Construction) written in the eleventh century by Tachibana no Toshitsuna and dealing with how to re-create nature in the small space of a garden and another fifteenth century text that illustrates how to employ the various elements-rock, water, plants —— and how to elicit a mood or atmosphere from a garden. Other way in which this tradition has been passed on are through the oral transmission from teacher to apprentice, through the actual physical labor of serving as an apprentice, through learning from nature and finally, by viewing the gardens of past designers. [See, Japanese Gardens, Slawson].

The gardens that you see in these pages are obviously different from the vegetable or flower variety of garden that might come to mind on hearing the word "garden." They also differ in scale and symmetry from, for example, the grand type of garden-park we might find in Europe or in America. The gardens you are looking at are landscape gardens, although "nature-scape" gardens would perhaps be a more accurate expression, because they have been designed on a micro-scale to depict nature as it appears on a macro-scale. Or, to put it more simply, they are designed to depict the way the natural elements of rock, water and plant life actually appear in nature. In certain cases, when the designer set out a pine tree in the garden, he may likely have had Matsushima or Amanohashidate (two famous scenic sites in Japan) in the back of his mind. Compare a view of Amanohashidate with the garden at Katsura Rikyū (the Detached Villa at Katsura) and you will readily see the intention of the designer. The intentional depiction of some famous natural landscape in Japan (or China) can be seen in many of the stroll gardens. The stroll gardens with or without ponds were constructed so that the viewers actually took a turn around the pond (read "lake" or "ocean" here) with the intention of visiting, vicariously, of course, far away places. When it was first built, the pond at **Kinkaku-ji** was undoubtedly enjoyed in such a way.

Although it is admittedly not altogether fair to try to formulate the principles of Japanese garden design in Western terms, one might say that, generally speaking, while the stroll and pond gardens seem to have been designed to be enjoyed for their own sakes (art for the sake of art, beauty for beauty's sake), the dry nature-scape gardens, *karesansui*, the prominent style of the Zen gardens, tend to be more didactic or symbolic. That is, there is an intention to build into the design and construction something to show or teach us.

One of the earliest dry nature-scape gardens, **Daisen-in** (photos #6 and #7), for example, seems almost like a story readable with the eyes —— the water flowing down the mountains, extending outward at the base, flowing under a bridge, and on out into the southern garden "ocean." Actually, this particular garden is often considered by garden design scholars as a transitional one incorporating the elements of nature —— waterfall, river, a Chinese *junk,* (don't ask me what the Chinese *junk* is doing there) while at the same time, draws our sensual response.

The question that arises is: is the emphasis on the realistic "objective" depiction of nature or is it intended more to elicit a subjective sensual response of the viewer? In other words, the two most fundamental principles of garden making, one, the re-creation of natural habitat and, two, the attempt to appeal to the less rational and more intuitive sense of the viewer, are both embodied here.

There is really no right or wrong answer to the question I posed above concerning whether a particular garden has been an attempt to objectively recreate a natural phenomenon or whether the designer was intending to more poetically depict some universal motif. It is simply my intention to formulate a question that arose in my mind and hope that it might stimulate the viewers of these gardens to take a more active role in observing them in order to have a more enriching experience.

In any event, whether the garden was intended to be enjoyed for its own inherent qualities with little or no connection to teaching us something or whether it was intended to show us some deep philosophical truth or to represent a particular Buddhist, Taoist, Shintoist, or Confucian motif, I think it would be agreed upon by most people that these gardens certainly take our minds away from the paltry cares of the day and serve to open us up to taking another look at our lives from a wider perspective.

Glossary

● Bakufu

The feudal military government in Japan from the Kamakura period through the Edo or Tokugawa period. Headed by a *shôgun* or military general. After the fall of the aristocracy that saw the end of the Heian period successive shogunates were led by certain powerful families. The Hôjô line held power during the Kamakura period eventually giving way to the Ashikaga line who brought the seat of government back to Kyoto.

● Bodai-ji

A temple usually established by a single high ranking family. As opposed to a *dannadera* or temple supported by many families.

● Bodhisattva

Strictly speaking, it refers to a limited number of Buddhist saints such as Kannon Bosatsu or Bodhisattva of All-seeing-and-hearing. More broadly speaking, anyone who takes a vow to save all sentient beings is a bodhisattva. Popularly speaking, a bodhisattva is the ideal human role model.

● Chisenkaiyu

A type of garden viewed from various vantage points while strolling around the path.

● Gozan

Literally meaning "five mountains," it refers to the system of ranking temples during feudal Japan. Originally, there were five *gozan* or top ranking temples in Kamakura and five in Kyoto. The *gozan* served to introduce Zen into Japan as well as Chinese literature and the arts. It also helped the *bakufu* governments to keep a tight control on the activities of the temples. Those belonging to the *gozan* today are **Nanzen-ji, Tôfuku-ji, Kennin-ji, Shôkoku-ji,** and

Tenryû-ji.

● Hôjô

The abbot's quarters. The size of the *hôjô* varied with the size of the temple although originally, they were about ten square feet which is what the word literally means, a ten foot square hut.

● Mt. Hôrai

Narrowly speaking, it refers to a particular type of rock formation symbolically depicting the dwelling place of the ancient Chinese sages. A garden with this type of rock formation is sometimes called a "*hôrai* garden."

● Ichimatsu moyo

A checkered pattern made of stones and moss found at **Tôfuku-ji.**

● Jissatsu

The second tier for ranking Zen temples. The *gozan* or "five mountains" comprised the top layer. The *jissatsu* or "ten temples" comprised the second layer.

● Kaisandô

A building in which the ashes of the founder of a temple are enshrined.

● Karamon

A Chinese-style gate usually much more ornate than the Japanese style.

● Karesansui

A dry landscape garden utilizing a minimum number of natural elements, generally speaking, only rocks, white sand and moss or shrubbery. This style garden expresses the Zen preference for simplicity —— the idea of doing the most with the least.

● Karetaki

Literally, dry-waterfall, depicted either by white sand or by a rock with vertical fissures simulating water.

A common motif in the dry landscape garden.

● Kensho

A Zen term that refers to seeing into one's original nature.

● Kôan

In Rinzai Zen, a rationally insolvable problem given to the student to meditate on during zazen and at other times during the day. The teacher prods and guides the student until he or she is forced to make a psychological breakthrough.

● Kito

A sort of prayer or invocation requesting some benefit, for example, peace in the country, protection from one's enemies, or victory in battle. On the individual scale, *kito* prayers are offered for the soul of an aborted infant or one who might have died in childbirth.

● Matsu-ji

A branch or subordinate temple of a larger temple, perhaps one founded by a disciple of a teacher of a large temple somewhere in a different part of the country. As opposed to a *tatchû* which is usually located on the grounds of the larger temple and supported by one or only a few wealthy families.

● Munen musô

Mistakenly thought to imply that zazen is a special state which the practitioner arrives at whereby there are no thoughts or perceptions. In practical terms it means practicing letting go of one's petty home spun ideas and opinions over and over again.

● Nakaniwa

A garden enclosed on all sides by buildings or verandas.

● Namu Amida Butsu

An invocation or expression of giving oneself up to Amida Buddha.

● Nembutsu

The name given to the item above.

● Rinzai school of Zen

One of the original "five houses" or lineages of Zen that developed in China during the Tang dynasty and later was introduced into Japan by Myôan Eisai and Enni Ben'en.

● Rojiniwa

Sometimes simply, *roji*. The path and garden leading to a teahouse.

● Sanson iwagumi

A garden motif composed of three rocks, the central of which is the largest, symbolizing Amida Buddha surrounded by Kannon and Seishi Bodhisattvas, or sometimes Shakyamuni Buddha attended by two saints, or Yakushi Nyorai, the buddha of medicine, flanked by Nikkô Bosatsu (the bodhisattva of sunlight) and Gekkô Bosatsu (the bodhisattva of moonlight).

● Satori

A very deep realization of one's self nature or original nature.

● Shikantaza

Literally, it means "just sitting." *Shikantaza* is the type of zazen taught by Eihei Dôgen Zenji. Also translated as "concentrated sitting" or themeless-sitting. As opposed to visualization meditation or *kôan* Zen.

● Shôen

Landed estates scattered throughout Japan during its medieval history. Many were owned by absentee nobles or members of the court. Their ownership changed hands, at times quite frequently, as they were given as a reward or taken away as a punishment at the will of the *shôgun* or emperor.

● Shoin

The *shoin* was a large room or hall used by the monks for study. Later, it came to be used as a room or building for special guests. *Shoinzukuri*, or *shoin* style architecture was employed largely by the samurai class.

● Sôdô

A building for monks to live in and do zazen. The *sôdô* was not one of the original buildings in Buddhist monasteries, but became one of the key building with the development and influence of Zen.

● Sôhei

Literally, "soldier-monks." The *sôhei* on Mt. Hiei or Mt. Kôya helped protect their respective monastic complexes from outside "enemies," as well as took periodic forays into Kyoto to burn it down on occasions when imperial or shogunal decrees went against their interests or when the emperor or *shôgun* showed special favor towards the Zen monasteries.

● Sôroku

A secular bureau within the monasteries "responsible for the appointment and promotion of abbots and monastic officers, collection of fees, ranking of monasteries, granting of monastic domain, and maintenance of standards of monastic life. "(See Five Mountains, Collcutt.)

● Sôtô school of Zen

Brought from China by Eihei Dôgen (1200-1253) around 1228. One of the original "five houses" or lineages of Chinese Zen. Emphasizes *shikantaza* or "just sitting," as opposed to Rinzai Zen which empha

sizes the study of *kôan*. The two *honzan* or head-temples are **Eihei-ji** in Fukui Prefecture and **Sôji-ji** located in Tsurumi, near Yokohama.

● Sôzu

A bamboo device that fills with water and then empties with a sharp crack when it hits a rock. The *sôzu* were used to frighten deer.

● Tanzaku

A rectangularly shaped strip of paper for writting a poem on. Small ones are used for writting a prayer on and then folded and attached to the lower branches of trees in shrines. Long narrow stones in the *tanzaku* shape were laid as bridges in landscape gardens.

● Tenzo

The cook of the monastery in charge of not only the preparation of meals but of acquiring all the ingredients and their disposal as well.

● Tsuboniwa

A *tsubo* is a pot, so a *tsuboniwa* implies a very small garden not much larger than a pot.

● Tsukiyama

An artificially built mound of sand or soil employed in garden design to symbolize a mountain. The soil often came from the soil that was removed to make the pond.

● Tsurukame

Literally, a crane and tortoise. The *tsurukame* motif is used frequently in garden design. The *tsuru* (crane) is the erect stone of the pair, while the *kame* (tortoise) is the horizontal or flat stone. They both symbolize longevity and wisdom.

● Tsurushima

A "crane" island. The vertical rock in the *tsurukame* motif.

At a glance

	Temple	Founded	Fees and Hours
○Daitoku-ji			
1. 2	Daitoku-ji	1319	Closed to the public
3. 4. 5	Ryôgen-in	1504	¥350 9:00 ～ 4:30
6. 7	Daisen-in	1509	¥400 9:00 ～ 5:00
8	Kôtô-in	1603	¥300 9:00 ～ 4:00
9. 10	Kohô-an	1621	Closed to the public
11. 12	Hôshun-in	1608	Closed to the public
13	Jukô-in	1582	Closed to the public
14	Zuihô-in	1541	¥300 9:00 ～ 5:00
15. 16	Shûon-an	1456	¥400 9:00 ～ 5:00
○Myôshin-ji			
17. 18	Taizô-in	1404	¥400 9:00 ～ 5:00
19. 20	Tôkai-an	1484	Closed to the public
21	Keishun-in	1598	¥400 8:00 ～ 4:00
22	Tôrin-in	1556	Closed to the public
23. 24	Ryôan-ji	1499	¥400 8:00 ～ 5:00
○Shôkoku-ji			
25	Kinkaku-ji	1395	¥400 9:00 ～ 5:30
26	Ginkaku-ji	1480	¥500 8:30 ～ 5:00
○Nanzen-ji			
27	Nanzen-in		¥150 8:30 ～ 4:30
28	Nanzen-ji	1290	¥350 8:30 ～ 4:30
29	Tenju-an		¥300 9:00 ～ 5:00
30	Konchi-in	1632	¥400 8:30 ～ 4:30

	Temple	Founded	Fees and Hours
○Tôfuku-ji			
31. 32	Tôfuku-ji	1236	¥300 9:00 ～ 4:00
33	Sesshû-ji	1321	¥300 9:00 ～ 5:00
34	Tentoku-in		Closed to the public
○Kennin-ji			
35	Entoku-in	1607	Closed to the public
36	Kôdai-ji	1605	¥500 9:00 ～ 4:00
○Tenryû-ji			
37. 38	Tenryû-ji	1339	¥500 8:30 ～ 5:00
39. 40	Tôji-in	1341	¥400 8:00 ～ 5:00
41. 42. 43	Saihô-ji	1339	By appointment
44	Jizô-in	1367	¥400 9:00 ～ 5:00
○			
45	Shôden-ji	1268	¥300 9:00 ～ 5:00
46	Konpuku-ji		¥300 9:00 ～ 5:00
47	Shisen-do		¥400 9:00 ～ 5:00

The visitor's fees listed here are as of September 1, 1994

72

Information

To enjoy your limited vacation time in Kyoto, it's a good idea to visit the Tourist Information Center just across and up the street (Karasuma Dori, west side) from Kyoto Station's Central Exit. There is a Japanese staff who will be most helpful and, in English. The Information Center will provide, free of charge, detailed information on transportation, lodging, meals, sightseeing, etc. In addition, the staff will be most helpful answering any questions you might have regarding such diverse topics as traditional crafts and local products, history, or local church services. The Center also has a supply of introductory pamphlets on other cities and areas of Japan.

● Tourist Information Center, Kyoto Office
Kyoto Tower Bldg., 1st Floor, Shichijo Karasuma-sagaru, Kyoto.
Tel: 075(371)5649 Hours: 9:00a.m.–5:00p.m. Closed. Saturday afternoons, Sundays and National holidays. Free telephone service: When calling from outside Kyoto, between 9:00a.m.–5:00p.m., please call the following toll-free number for information on events in Kansai: 0120–444–800. This free service is available every day of the year. For information on events in Tokyo, call: 0120–222–800.

When traveling within Kyoto City by the Municipal Bus (in Japanese, shiei bus) or Municipal Subway lines, the "one-day pass" is most economical. One adult pass for ¥1,050 entitles the user to unlimited boarding privileges for the local bus and subway, as well as the Kyoto Bus Line (a private company). For most destinations in the city, the bus fare is ¥180, the subway, ¥160–¥250. The MK Taxi service is convenient for the foreign tourist as there are a number of drivers quite fluent in English. Tel: 075(721)2237. The first two kilometers cost ¥470, ¥80 for each additional 500 meters.

For news and information on what is going on in the Kyoto-Osaka-Kobe area (commonly called Kansai or Kinki) two fine magazines published in English are "Kansai Time Out" (a monthly at ¥300) and "Kyoto Journal" (a quarterly at ¥500). Two publications in English, KYOTO: Seven Paths to the Heart of the City (¥1,500) and Old Kyoto (¥1,800) will introduce you to several wonderful walking routes through the city and some 80 craft shops, restaurants, and inns, etc. All of these publications are available at either Avanti Book Center on the 6th floor of the Avanti Building opposite the Hachijo-guchi Exit (the south exit) of Kyoto Station, or on the 3rd floor of Maruzen Bookstore on Kawaramachi between Shijo and Sanjo-dori, as well as at most hotels where foreign tourists might stay. At the above two bookstores there are some English speaking staff to help you. Both stores also carry many other books in English and other languages.

Historical Periods and Prominent Garden Styles

- Heian Period (794~1185)

Large pond gardens to match *shinden zukuri*, or palace style architecture. Viewed either while strolling or by boat.

- Kamakura Period (1185~1333)

Pond gardens for strolling through, employing more rocks and stones.

- Nanbokucho Period (1336~1392)

Southern Northern dynasties period. Dry landscape gardens.

- Muromachi Period (1334~1568)

Zen influenced dry landscape gardens and large pond gardens.

- Momoyama Period (1568~1603)

Castle building period when garden design incorporated massive rocks and stonework.

- Tokugawa period or Edo Period (1603~1868)

Synthesis of pond gardens and *roji*.

- Meiji period (1868~1912)

Inovation in garden design.

- Taisho period (1912~1926)
- Showa period (1926~1989)
- Heisei period (1989~   )

Books

- A Guide to the Gardens of Kyoto
  Treib, M. Herman, Shufunotomo Co. Ltd.,Tokyo, 1980
- Five Mountains
  M. Collcutt, Harvard, 1981
- Invitation to Japanese Gardens
  K. Asano, G. Takakuwa, R.F.Dickinson, N. Matsuyama, Tuttle, 1970
- Invitation to Kyoto Gardens
  K. Yamamoto, T. Wright, Y. Asano, M. Takagi, Mitsumura Suiko Shoin, 1989
- Historical Kyoto
  H. Plutschow, The Japan Times, 1983
- Japanese Gardens
  D. Slawson, Kodansha, 1987

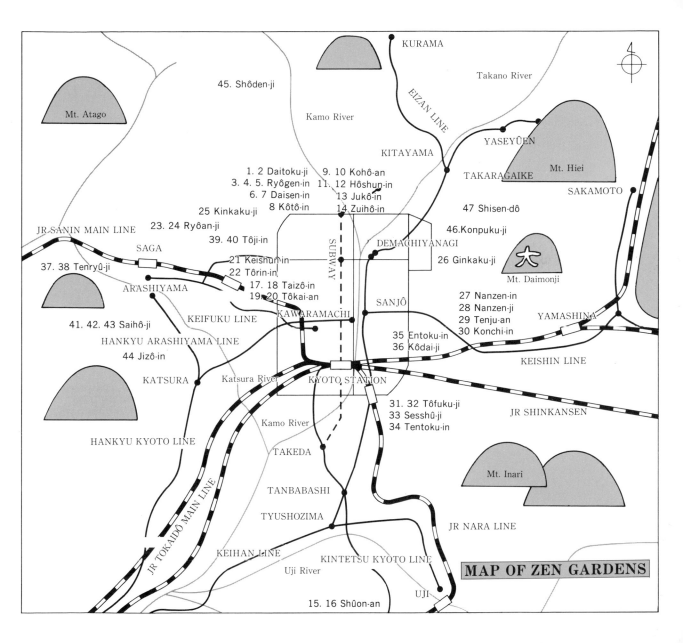

MAP OF ZEN GARDENS

About the Author

Tom Wright, born in Racine and raised in Watertown, Wisconsin, first came to Japan in 1967. After spending two years in Hokkaido and three more in Kyoto studying Zen at Antai-ji temple, he returned to Wisconsin, graduating in 1987 in Japanese Studies. In 1974, Mr.Wright was ordained as a priest in the Sôtô school of Zen and continued his study and practice of Buddhism under Kôshô Uchiyama Rôshi. He is presently a full-time instructor at Ryûkoku University in Kyoto.

Mr. Wright co-translated Approach to Zen, a text on zazen written by Uchiyama Rôshi, and later translated the "Tenzô Kyôkun" of Eihei Dôgen Zenji, along with a modern-day commentary on it by Uchiyama Rôshi, under the title, Refining Your Life, (Weatherhill, 1983). He assisted in the translation and editing of Shikantaza, an introductory book on zazen published by the Kyoto Sôtô Zen Center, and with the editing and style of the Shôbôgenzô Zuimonki, also published by the Kyoto Sôtô Zen Center.

Mr. Wright also translated the text for the first book in this series, Invitation to Kyoto Gardens,a Suiko Books publication in 1989.

About the Photographer

Mizuno Katsuhiko was born in Kyoto in 1941. Since 1969 he has been working to capture the beauties of the various natural scenery and landscapes of this city with his camera. Among his over thirteen publications are : Kyoto Tsubo Niwa (Miniature Gardens), published by Mitsumura Suiko Shoin, in 1980; Kyoto no Tsubaki to Tera (Kyoto's Temples and Camelias), published by Nihon Shashin Kikaku, in 1981 ; Shiki Kyoto (The Four Seasons of Kyoto), published by Mitsumura Suiko Shoin, in 1983 ; Kyoto Hanameisho Shirizu (A Collection of Well-known Places for Flowers in Kyoto), Sakura (Cherries), Shiki no Hana (Flowers of the Seasons), Kôyô (Autumn Leaves), Kachô Fûgetsu (The Beauties of Nature), and Hyakka Ryôran (Bursting With Flowers), all published by Kyoto Shoin, in 1986~1987, as well as the Meitei Saijiki Shirizu (The Gardens of Kyoto) Kyoto ─── Kurashi no Niwa (The Gardens of the City Dweller), published by Kyoto Shoin, in 1987.

Mr. Mizuno has also written numerous editorials on traditional Japanese culture. He is also a member of the Japan Photographers Association.